Listening

with *Blessed*
John Paul II

Listening to God

with *Blessed* John Paul II

Compiled by
AMY WELBORN

Our Sunday Visitor Publishing Division
Our Sunday Visitor, Inc.
Huntington, Indiana 46750

ISBN: 978-1-59276-303-0 (Inventory No. T1196)
LCCN: 2011923163

Cover design: Rebecca J. Heaston
Cover photo: Catholic Press Photo
Interior design: Sherri L. Hoffman

PRINTED IN THE UNITED STATES OF AMERICA

CONTENTS

INTRODUCTION

"BE NOT AFRAID!"

It was with these words that Pope John Paul II began his papacy in October of 1978. The call to move forward and to embrace discipleship with joy and courage emerged almost naturally from the dramatic course of Karol Wotyla's life.

When we think of what it means to "listen to God," we often focus on how to discern the Lord's voice in our moments of intentional, focused prayer. What we can learn from Blessed John Paul II is the importance of expanding our understanding and of developing that attentive stance not only for quiet moments but also for the course of everyday life, in all of its noise, confusion, and complexity.

For this is what Karol Wotyla did. Growing into adulthood, the priesthood was really not on his mind. He was involved in theater and various types of activism. But when his life, along with the lives of all the Polish people, was swept up first in the ravages of war and later in the looming specter of Communist tyranny, he heard, in the sufferings and oppression of his brothers and sisters, God calling him to a different path. And he listened.

In the selections in this book — taken from homilies, General Audience talks, addresses, and other writings — Pope John Paul II reminds us that before we can understand what God is saying to us, we must first embrace our identity as children of God. We listen first to God's word, which tells us the truth about who we are, and we listen to Christ, who gives us the Good News of God's redeeming love for each one of us.

Rooted in that faith in God's love for us, we can then approach our daily lives, in every one of our particular life's circumstances, confident that God is speaking to us there and open to what he has to say. Pope John Paul II reminds all of us in these selections — young people, men and women, married, single, the elderly, artists — of God's constant presence in our lives, his continual whisper in our hearts.

It is in listening to God that we live most fully — the way we were created to live. God's love for us, whom he has created for love eternal with him, echoes through these selections, perhaps most succinctly expressed by the Holy Father in his invitation to university students in 1979: "Allow him to find you!" — a powerful invitation for all of us, no matter what age or stage in life we may find ourselves.

— AMY WELBORN

1. Do Not Be Afraid

THE NEW SUCCESSOR OF PETER in the See of Rome today makes a fervent, humble, and trusting prayer: Christ, make me become and remain the servant of your unique power, the servant of your sweet power, the servant of your power that knows no eventide. Make me be a servant. Indeed, the servant of your servants.

Brothers and sisters, do not be afraid to welcome Christ and accept his power. Help the Pope and all those who wish to serve Christ and with Christ's power to serve the human person and the whole of mankind. Do not be afraid. Open wide the doors for Christ.

> — *Homily at the Inauguration of His Pontificate*
> (October 22, 1978)

"Do not let your hearts be troubled or afraid."

> — JOHN 14:27

2. KNOWING YOURSELF

THE MAN WHO WISHES to understand himself thoroughly —
and not just in accordance with immediate, partial, often su-
perficial, and even illusory standards and measures of his being
— he must with his unrest, uncertainty, and even his weakness
and sinfulness, with his life and death, draw near to Christ.
He must, so to speak, enter into him with all his own self, he
must "appropriate" and assimilate the whole of the reality of
the Incarnation and Redemption in order to find himself....

In reality, the name for that deep amazement at man's worth
and dignity is the Gospel, that is to say: the Good News.

— *Redemptor Hominis*, n. 10
(encyclical, March 4, 1979)

Probe me, God, know my heart;
try me, know my concerns.

— PSALM 139:23

3. SONS AND DAUGHTERS OF GOD

I REMEMBER A SONG I used to sing in Poland as a young man, a song which I still sing as Pope, which tells about the birth of the Savior. On Christmas night, in every church and chapel, this song would ring out, repeating in a musical way the story told in the Gospel. It says: "In the silence of the night, a voice is heard: 'Get up, shepherds, God is born for you! Hurry to Bethlehem to meet the Lord.'" The same story is told in the beautiful hymn "Silent Night," which everyone knows. That is a hymn which moves us deeply by reminding us that Jesus, the Son of God, was born of Mary, born to make us holy and to make us adopted sons and daughters of God. It is a hymn to the creative power of the Holy Spirit. It is a song to help us not to be afraid.

— *Homily, Mass With Young People, New York City*
(October 7, 1995)

For those who are led by the Spirit of God are children of God. For you did not receive a spirit of slavery to fall back into fear, but you received a spirit of adoption, through which we cry, "Abba, Father!"
— ROMANS 8:14-15

4. SPEAKING TO GOD

To pray means speaking to God — I would venture to say even more — to pray means finding oneself again in that One eternal Word through which the Father speaks, and which speaks to the Father. This Word became flesh, so that it would be easier for us to find ourselves again in him even with our human word of prayer. This word may sometimes be very imperfect, sometimes we may even lack it, but this incapacity of our human words is continually completed in the Word that became flesh in order to speak to the Father with the fullness of that mystical union which every man who prays forms with him, which all those who pray form with him.

— *General Audience*
(March 14, 1979)

In the same way, the Spirit too comes to the aid of our weakness; for we do not know how to pray as we ought, but the Spirit itself intercedes with inexpressible groanings.

— ROMANS 8:26

5. Teach Us to Pray

WHEN, IN ANSWER TO the request of the disciples "teach us to pray," Christ utters the words of his prayer, he teaches not only the words, but he teaches that in our talk with the Father there must be complete sincerity and full openness. Prayer must embrace everything that is part of our life. It cannot be something additional or marginal. Everything must find in it its true voice. Even everything that burdens us; things of which we are ashamed; what by its very nature separates us from God. This above all. It is prayer that always, first of all and essentially, demolishes the barrier which sin and evil may have raised between us and God.

— *General Audience*
(March 14, 1979)

He was praying in a certain place, and when he had finished, one of his disciples said to him, "Lord, teach us to pray just as John taught his disciples."

— LUKE 11:1

6. LED BY THE SPIRIT

THE SPIRIT WHO DWELLS in the Church also abides in the heart of every member of the faithful: he is the *dulcis hospes animae* [sweet guest of the soul]. Following a path of conversion and personal sanctification, then, means allowing ourselves to be "led" by the Spirit, letting him act, pray, and love in us. "Becoming holy" is possible if we allow ourselves to be made holy by him who is the Holy One, by docilely co-operating with his transforming action....

We can think of the Holy Spirit as the *soul* of our soul, and thus the secret of our sanctification. Let us dwell in his powerful and discreet, intimate and transforming presence!

— *General Audience*
(July 8, 1998)

"But when he comes, the Spirit of truth, he will guide you to all truth."
— JOHN 16:13

7. BECOMING WHO WE ARE

CHRISTIAN SPIRITUALITY DOES NOT consist in an effort to *perfect oneself,* as if man could further his overall personal growth and achieve salvation by his own strength. The human heart, wounded by sin, is healed only by the grace of the Holy Spirit, and only if sustained by this grace can man live as a true son of God.

Nor does Christian spirituality consist in becoming "immaterial," disembodied as it were, without responsible involvement in human affairs. Indeed, the Holy Spirit's presence in us, far from urging us to seek an alienating "escape," penetrates and moves our entire being: intellect, will, emotions, and bodily nature, so that our "new nature" will imbue space and time with the newness of the Gospel.

— *General Audience*
(October 21, 1998)

You should put away the old self of your former way of life, corrupted through deceitful desires, and be renewed in the spirit of your minds, and put on the new self, created in God's way in righteousness and holiness of truth.

— EPHESIANS 4:22-24

8. REAL LOVE

THE SADNESS OF THE young man makes us reflect. We could be tempted to think that many possessions, many of the goods of this world, can bring happiness. We see instead in the case of the young man in the Gospel that his many possessions had become an obstacle to accepting the call of Jesus to follow him. He was not ready to say *yes* to Jesus and *no* to self, to say *yes* to love and *no* to escape.

Real love is demanding. It means discipline and sacrifice, but it also means joy and human fulfillment.

— *Homily, Mass on Boston Commons, Boston*
(October 1, 1979)

Jesus said to him, "If you wish to be perfect, go, sell what you have and give to [the] poor, and you will have treasure in heaven. Then come, follow me."

— MATTHEW 19:21

9. PRAYING IN CHRIST

OUR PRAYER BECOMES A school of love — a special kind of Christian consecrated love, by which we love the world, but with the heart of Christ.

Through this prayer of Christ to which we give voice, our day is sanctified, our activities transformed, our actions made holy. We pray the same psalms that Jesus prayed, and come into personal contact with him — the person to whom all Scripture points, the goal to which all history is directed.

In our celebration of the word of God, the mystery of Christ opens up before us and envelops us. And through union with our Head, Jesus Christ, we become ever more increasingly one with all the members of his Body.

— *Address, Morning Prayer at St. Patrick's Cathedral, New York City* (October 3, 1979)

He is before all things,
and in him all things hold together.
He is the head of the body, the church.

— COLOSSIANS 1:17–18

10. THE TRIUMPH OF THE CROSS

CHRIST *IS* THE LORD! This will be confirmed in the Resurrection, but it is *already* contained in the *Crucifixion*. Precisely in the Crucifixion.

To be crucified, humanly speaking, is to be disgraced and humiliated. But from God's point of view it means being lifted up, indeed, to be lifted up by means of the cross. Christ is the Lord, and he becomes Lord of everything and everyone in this elevation by means of the cross. It is in this way that we look upon the cross, with the eyes of faith, *instructed by the word of God*, guided by the power of God.

Here then is the mystery of *the Triumph of the Cross.*

— *Homily, Mass at Arizona State University, Phoenix*
(September 14, 1987)

The message of the cross is foolishness to those who are perishing, but to us who are being saved it is the power of God.

— 1 CORINTHIANS 1:18

11. GIVING GOD OUR TIME

D0 NOT BE AFRAID *to give your time to Christ!* Yes, let us open our time to Christ, that he may cast light upon it and give it direction. He is the One who knows the secret of time and the secret of eternity, and he gives us "his day" as an ever-new gift of his love.... Time given to Christ is never time lost, but is rather time gained, so that our relationships and indeed our whole life may become more profoundly human.

— *Dies Domini*, n. 7
(apostolic letter, May 31, 1998)

Jesus said to them, "Come after me, and I will make you fishers of men." Then they abandoned their nets and followed him.

— MARK 1:17-18

12. BODY OF CHRIST

LET US REMEMBER THAT the place of Christ's presence on earth was not only the Upper Room in Jerusalem, but also the streets of towns and country roads. Everywhere people gathered before him. They gathered together to be able to be with him, to listen to him.

In the solemnity of Corpus Christi this particular presence of Christ in the streets, squares, and by the wayside, is renewed. He speaks to us who have gathered, not with the living words of the Gospel, as he once did, but with the eloquent silence of the Eucharist.

— *Angelus*
(June 17, 1979)

Jesus said to them, "I am the bread of life; whoever comes to me will never hunger, and whoever believes in me will never thirst."

— JOHN 6:35

13. BECOME LIKE A CHILD

WHAT DOES IT MEAN that "unless you turn and become like children, you will not enter the kingdom of heaven" (Matthew 18:3)? *Is not Jesus pointing to children as models* even for grown-ups? In children there is something that must never be missing in people who want to enter the kingdom of heaven. People who are destined to go to heaven are simple like children, and like children are full of trust, rich in goodness, and pure. Only people of this sort can find in God a Father and, thanks to Jesus, can become in their own turn children of God.

— *Letter to Children in the Year of the Family*
(December 13, 1994)

"Whoever humbles himself like this child is the greatest in the kingdom of heaven."

— MATTHEW 18:4

14. THE PASSAGE OF TIME

DEAR BROTHERS AND SISTERS, at our age it is natural to revisit the past in order to attempt a sort of assessment.... The passage of time helps us to see our experiences in a clearer light and softens their painful side. Sadly, struggles and tribulations are very much a part of everyone's life. Sometimes it is a matter of problems and sufferings which can sorely test our mental and physical resistance, and perhaps even shake our faith. But experience teaches that daily difficulties, by God's grace, often contribute to people's growth and to the forging of their character.

— *Letter to the Elderly*
(October 1, 1999)

So with old age is wisdom,
and with length of
days understanding.

— JOB 12:12

15. In Beauty, We See God

Beauty is a key to the mystery and a call to transcendence. It is an invitation to savor life and to dream of the future. That is why the beauty of created things can never fully satisfy. It stirs that hidden nostalgia for God which a lover of beauty like St. Augustine could express in incomparable terms: "Late have I loved you, beauty so old and so new: late have I loved you!" (*Confessions*, 10, 27: CCL 27, 251).

Artists of the world, may your many different paths all lead to that infinite Ocean of beauty where wonder becomes awe, exhilaration, unspeakable joy.

— *Letter to Artists*
(April 4, 1999)

The heavens declare the glory of God;
the sky proclaims its builder's craft.

— Psalm 19:2

16. A REASON FOR HOPE

BUT WHEN WE LOOK closely at the real situation of each person, forced to confront his own frailty and loneliness, we realize that, more than we think, hearts are weighed down by anguish, by worry about the future, by fear of sickness and death....

Christianity offers no cheap comforts, demanding as it is in requiring an authentic faith and a strict moral life. But it gives us reason for *hope* by showing us God as a *Father rich in mercy* who has given us his Son, thereby revealing to us his immense love.

— *Angelus*
(March 9, 1997)

"While he was still a long way off, his father caught sight of him, and was filled with compassion. He ran to his son, embraced him and kissed him."

— LUKE 15:20

17. TRUE PEACE

PEACE BE WITH YOU! It is not only a greeting but a gift. Jesus assures us that peace is possible, because he gives us both its secret and its strength. He comes to dislodge us from that comfortable pessimism which sometimes makes us think that war and violence are inevitable, and to take refuge in our own security and borders, as if the suffering of distant brothers and sisters did not pertain to us and we could rightly abandon them to their own destiny. No, this is not so! The peace offered by Christ is *a duty incumbent on us all* and commits us to having a truly "*universal*" heart.

— *Regina Caeli*
(April 6, 1997)

Jesus came and stood in their midst and said to them, "Peace be with you."

— JOHN 20:19

18. LET GOD BE GOD

IT IS POSSIBLE, in fact, to know Holy Scripture perfectly, it is possible to be learned in philosophy and in theology, yet not have faith, or fail in faith; because it is always God who calls first to know him and love him in the right way. It is necessary, therefore, to be humble before the Almighty.

It is necessary to maintain the sense of mystery, because there always remains the infinite between God and man. It is necessary to remember that before God and his Revelation it is not so much a question of understanding with one's own limited reason, but rather of loving.

— *Address to Students*
(March 24, 1979)

Teach me, LORD, your way
that I may walk in your truth,
single-hearted and revering your name.

— PSALM 86:11

19. Dependence on God

Prayer is in fact the recognition of our limitation and our dependence: we come from God, we belong to God and we return to God! We cannot, therefore, but abandon ourselves to him, our Creator and Lord, with full and complete confidence....

Thus, reflecting on the nature of the universe and on our own life, we understand and recognize that we are creatures, limited and yet sublime, who owe their existence to the Infinite Majesty of the Creator!

Prayer, therefore, is first of all an act of intelligence, a feeling of humility and gratitude, an attitude of trust and abandonment to him who gave us life out of love.

— *Address to Young People*
(March 14, 1979)

Blessed is the man who trusts in the LORD,
whose hope is the LORD.
He is like a tree planted beside the waters
that stretches out its roots to the stream.

— JEREMIAH 17:7-8

20. Our Bodies, Redeemed

Mary's Assumption reveals the nobility and dignity of the human body.

In the face of the profanation and debasement to which modern society frequently subjects the female body, the mystery of the Assumption proclaims the supernatural destiny and dignity of every human body, called by the Lord to become an instrument of holiness and to share in his glory.

Mary entered into glory because she welcomed the Son of God in her virginal womb and in her heart. By looking at her, the Christian learns to discover the value of his own body and to guard it as a temple of God, in expectation of the resurrection.

— *General Audience*
(July 9, 1997)

Do you not know that your body is a temple of the holy Spirit within you, whom you have from God, and that you are not your own?

For you have been purchased at a price. Therefore glorify God in your body.

— 1 Corinthians 6:19-20

21. GOD AND MAN FOR US

WE ARE CALLED TO assume this same attitude, walking on the way opened by the Son of God made man, so that we can share his journey to the Father. The eternity that enters into us is a sovereign power of love that seeks to guide our whole life to its ultimate purpose, hidden in the mystery of the Father.... Eternity has entered human life. Now human life is called to make the journey with Christ from time to eternity.

— *General Audience*
(December 10, 1997)

"I came from the Father and have come into the world. Now I am leaving the world and going back to the Father."

— JOHN 16:28

22. ALL FOR JESUS

CONTEMPLATING YOU, I THINK with trepidation and with trust of what is in store for you in life and of what you will be in the world of tomorrow, and I wish to leave you, as a viaticum for your lives, three thoughts:

— look for Jesus,
— love Jesus,
— bear witness to Jesus.

— Address to Youth
(November 8, 1978)

Now there were some Greeks among those who had come up to worship at the feast. They came to Philip, who was from Bethsaida in Galilee, and asked him, "Sir, we would like to see Jesus."

— JOHN 12:20-21

23. SOLIDARITY IN SUFFERING

I COUNT A GREAT DEAL on the prayer of the sick, on the intercession with God of those who are suffering. They are so near Christ! And I approach them, aware that Christ is present in them....

We must stop, then, in front of suffering, in front of suffering man, to rediscover this essential link between one's human "self" and his. We must stop before suffering man, to testify to him and, as far as possible, together with him, all the dignity of suffering, I would say all the majesty of suffering. We must bow our heads before brothers or sisters who are weak and helpless, deprived just of what has been granted to us to enjoy every day.

— *Angelus*
(February 11, 1979)

Blessed be the God and Father of our Lord Jesus Christ, the Father of compassion and God of all encouragement, who encourages us in our every affliction, so that we may be able to encourage those who are in any affliction with the encouragement with which we ourselves are encouraged by God.

— 2 CORINTHIANS 1:3–4

24. Be Humble

Bowing the head may be interpreted as a gesture of humiliation or resignation. Bowing the head before God is a sign of humility. Humility, however, is not identified with humiliation or resignation. It is not accompanied by faint-heartedness. On the contrary. Humility is creative submission to the power of truth and love. Humility is rejection of appearances and superficiality; it is the expression of the depth of the human spirit; it is the condition of its greatness.

St. Augustine, too, reminds us of this. In a sermon he says:... "Do you want to be great? Begin from the smallest thing. Do you intend to construct a large building, which rises up very high? Take into consideration in the first place the foundation of humility" (*Serm.* 69, 2; PL 38, 441).

— *Angelus*
(March 4, 1979)

"Rather, whoever wishes to be great among you shall be your servant; whoever wishes to be first among you shall be your slave. Just so, the Son of Man did not come to be served but to serve and to give his life as a ransom for many."

— Matthew 20:26-28

25. SEE HOW HE LOVES US

DEAR FRIENDS IN CHRIST: the love of God is so great that it goes *beyond the limits of human language*, beyond the grasp of artistic expression, beyond human understanding. And yet, it is *concretely embodied in God's Son, Jesus Christ*, and in his Body, the Church. God loves you! God loves you all, without distinction, without limit. . . .

In the spirit of St. Francis, then, I urge you all to open your hearts to God's love, to respond by your prayers and by the deeds of your lives. Let go of your doubts and fears, and let the mercy of God draw you to his heart. *Open the doors of your hearts* to our God who is rich in mercy.

— *Address at Mission Dolores Basilica, San Francisco*
(September 17, 1987)

For I am convinced that neither death, nor life, nor angels, nor principalities, nor present things, nor future things, nor powers, nor height, nor depth, nor any other creature will be able to separate us from the love of God in Christ Jesus our Lord.

— ROMANS 8:38–39

26. Go Out to All the World

At the beginning of this new century, our steps must quicken as we travel the highways of the world. Many are the paths on which each one of us and each of our Churches must travel, but there is no distance between those who are united in the same communion, the communion which is daily nourished at the table of the Eucharistic Bread and the Word of Life. Every Sunday, the Risen Christ asks us to meet him as it were once more in the Upper Room where, on the evening of "the first day of the week" (John 20:19) he appeared to his disciples in order to "breathe" on them his life-giving Spirit and launch them on the great adventure of proclaiming the Gospel.

— *Novo Millennio Ineunte*, n. 58
(apostolic letter, January 6, 2001)

When he had said this, he showed them his hands and his side. The disciples rejoiced when they saw the Lord. [Jesus] said to them again, "Peace be with you. As the Father has sent me, so I send you."

— John 20:20-21

27. Christ, the Beginning and the End

But if the life of each of us is limited and fragile, we are consoled by the thought that, by virtue of our spiritual souls, we will survive beyond death itself.... It is no coincidence that the Church, at the solemn Easter Vigil, uses the same two Greek letters in reference to Christ who lives yesterday, today, and forever: He is "the beginning and the end, Alpha and Omega. All time belongs to him and all the ages." Human experience, although subject to time, is set by Christ against the horizon of immortality. He "became a man among men, in order to join the beginning to the end, man to God" (St. Irenaeus of Lyons, *Adversus Haereses*, IV, 20, 4).

— *Letter to the Elderly*
(October 1, 1999)

"I am the Alpha and the Omega," says the Lord God, "the one who is and who was and who is to come, the almighty."

— Revelation 1:8

28. A BEING FOR LIFE

GOD'S MERCIFUL LOVE REGENERATES every human being; it is by accepting the gift of mercy from the Risen Lord that we can build a reconciled world, truly open to the horizons of life, of full and deep joy in the Triune God. After Easter, man is no longer a *being for death*, but a *being for life*. The abyss of death has been destroyed by the risen Christ's explosion of life.

... Jesus' glorification is a "premise" and "promise" of our glorification, as long as we do not refuse the gift of his merciful love by which we can participate in the Risen Christ's feast of life.

— *Regina Caeli*
(April 6, 1997)

For we are his handiwork, created in Christ Jesus for the good works that God has prepared in advance, that we should live in them.
— EPHESIANS 2:10

29. GET UP AND WALK

WHAT IS HOLINESS IF not entering into a deep relationship with God, Trinity of love, and growing in intimacy with Christ, Son of God incarnate? And does not true self-discipline contribute to strengthening the person's interior being as well as his integral growth?

Dear young people, Christ repeats to each one of you: "Get up and walk!" He counts on you, he awaits each one of you. He invites you to become aware of your dignity as persons for whom he shed his blood. He comes to meet you on the path of life; he forgives you and makes you a gift of his joy and his peace.

— *Angelus*
(August 3, 1997)

Peter said, "I have neither silver nor gold, but what I do have I give you: in the name of Jesus Christ the Nazorean, [rise and] walk."
— ACTS 3:6

30. The Mother of God

THE HISTORY OF CHRISTIAN piety teaches that Mary is the way which leads to Christ and that filial devotion to her takes nothing from intimacy with Jesus; indeed, it increases it and leads to the highest levels of perfection.

… Turning to her, drawn by her tenderness, the men and women of our time also meet Jesus, Savior and Lord of their lives.

Above all, the poor, tried in heart, in their affections and in their material need, find refuge and peace in the Mother of God, and discover that for all people true riches consist in the grace of conversion and of following Christ.

— *General Audience*
(May 7, 1997)

> *"My soul proclaims the greatness of the Lord;*
> *my spirit rejoices in God my savior.*
> *For he has looked upon his handmaid's lowliness;*
> *behold, from now on will all ages call me blessed."*

— LUKE 1:46-48

31. Freedom in the Spirit

THIS NEW HORIZON OF freedom created by the Spirit also guides our relationship with the brothers and sisters we meet on our way.

Precisely because Christ has freed me by his love and given me his Spirit, I can and must give myself freely in love to my neighbor. This profound truth is stated in the First Letter of the Apostle John: "By this we know love, that he laid down his life for us; and we ought to lay down our lives for the brethren" (1 John 3:16). Jesus' "new" commandment sums up the law of grace; the person who accepts it realizes his freedom to the full.

— *General Audience*
(September 2, 1998)

"This is my commandment: love one another as I love you. No one has greater love than this, to lay down one's life for one's friends."
— John 15:12-13

32. BE MESSENGERS OF JOY

BUT HOW MANY PEOPLE have never known this joy? ... And we need not look to the far ends of the earth for them. They live in our neighborhoods, they walk down our streets, they may even be members of our own families. They live without true joy because they live without hope. They live without hope because they have never heard, really heard the Good News of Jesus Christ, because they have never met a brother or a sister who touched their lives with the love of Jesus and lifted them up from their misery.

We must go to them therefore as messengers of hope.

— *Address in Harlem, New York*
(October 2, 1979)

Rejoice in the Lord always. I shall say it again: rejoice! Your kindness should be known to all. The Lord is near.

— PHILIPPIANS 4:4-5

33. MOVED TO LOVE

THE EUCHARIST SIGNIFIES this charity, and therefore recalls it, makes it present, and at the same time brings it about. Every time that we consciously share in it, there opens in our souls a real dimension of that unfathomable love that includes everything that God has done and continues to do for us human beings, as Christ says: "My Father goes on working, and so do I." Together with this unfathomable and free gift, which is charity revealed in its fullest degree in the saving sacrifice of the Son of God, the sacrifice of which the Eucharist is the indelible sign, there also springs up within us a lively response of love. We not only know love; we ourselves begin to love.

— *Dominicae Cenae*, n. 5
(apostolic exhortation, February 24, 1980)

"Whoever eats my flesh and drinks my blood remains in me and I in him."

— JOHN 6:56

34. WE WISH TO SEE JESUS

WE WISH TO SEE JESUS" (John 12:21). This request, addressed
to the apostle Philip by some Greeks who had made a pilgrimage to Jerusalem for the Passover, echoes spiritually in our ears
too during this Jubilee Year. Like those pilgrims of two thou-
sand years ago, the men and women of our own day — often
perhaps unconsciously — ask believers not only to "speak" of
Christ, but in a certain sense to "show" him to them. And is
it not the Church's task to reflect the light of Christ in every
historical period, to make his face shine also before the generations of the new millennium?

— *Novo Millennio Ineunte*, n. 16
(apostolic letter, January 6, 2001)

*Philip said to him, "Master, show us the Father, and that will be
enough for us."*

*Jesus said to him, "Have I been with you for so long a time and
you still do not know me, Philip? Whoever has seen me has seen the
Father."*

— JOHN 14:8-9

35. GOD SEEKS US

IN JESUS CHRIST God not only speaks to man but also *seeks him out*. The Incarnation of the Son of God attests that God goes in search of man. Jesus speaks of this search as the finding of a lost sheep. It is a search which *begins in the heart of God* and culminates in the Incarnation of the Word.... God therefore goes in search of man who *is his special possession* in a way unlike any other creature. Man is God's possession by virtue of a choice made in love: God seeks man out, moved by his fatherly heart.

— *Tertio Millennio Adveniente*, n. 7
(apostolic letter, November 10, 1994)

"What man among you having a hundred sheep and losing one of them would not leave the ninety-nine in the desert and go after the lost one until he finds it? And when he does find it, he sets it on his shoulders with great joy and, upon his arrival home, he calls together his friends and neighbors and says to them, 'Rejoice with me because I have found my lost sheep.'"

— LUKE 15:4–6

36. Seeing With God's Eyes

Going beyond our own frailties, we must turn to him, the one Teacher, sharing in his death so as to purify ourselves from that jealous attachment to feelings and memories, not of the great things God has done for us, but of the human affairs of a past that still weighs heavily on our hearts. May the Spirit clarify our gaze so that together we may reach out to contemporary man who is waiting for the good news. If we make a harmonious, illuminating, life-giving response to the world's expectations and sufferings, we will truly contribute to a more effective proclamation of the Gospel among the people of our time.

— *Orientale Lumen*, n. 4
(apostolic letter, May 2, 1995)

Jesus stopped and called them and said, "What do you want me to do for you?"

They answered him, "Lord, let our eyes be opened." Moved with pity, Jesus touched their eyes. Immediately they received their sight, and followed him.

— Matthew 20:32-34

37. MARY, MOTHER OF HOPE

MARY ALSO BECOMES A model of hope for the Church. In listening to the angel's message, the Virgin first directs her hope to the kingdom without end, which Jesus had been sent to establish.

She stands firm near the cross of her Son, waiting for the divine promise to be fulfilled. After Pentecost, the Mother of Jesus sustains the Church's hope despite the threat of persecution. She is thus the Mother of hope for the community of believers and for individual Christians, and she encourages and guides her children as they await the kingdom, supporting them in their daily trials and throughout the events of history, however tragic.

— *General Audience*
(September 3, 1997)

> *"He has thrown down the rulers from their thrones*
> *but lifted up the lowly.*
> *The hungry he has filled with good things;*
> *the rich he has sent away empty."*

— LUKE 1:52-53

38. SEEK HIM

WE MUST ALL LOOK for Jesus.

Very often we must look for him because we do not yet know him; at other times because we have lost him; and at other times, on the contrary, we look for him in order to know him better, to love him more, and to make him loved.

It can be said that man's whole life and the whole of human history is a great search for Jesus.

... We must not let ourselves be stopped by the difficulty; but like the shepherds of Bethlehem we must set out courageously and begin to search.

— *Address to Young People*
(December 27, 1978)

Seek the LORD while he may be found,
call him while he is near.

— ISAIAH 55:6

39. THE MYSTERY OF SUFFERING

SUFFERING IS ALSO A mysterious and overwhelming reality.

Well, we Christians, looking at the crucified Jesus, find the strength to accept this mystery. The Christian knows that, after original sin, human history is always a risk. But he also knows that God himself willed to enter our grief, feel our pangs, pass through the agony of the spirit and the torment of the body. Faith in Christ does not take away suffering, but illuminates it, raises it, purifies it, sublimates it, and makes it efficacious for eternity.

In any pain of ours, moral or physical, let us look at the Crucified! ... Only he can comfort and reassure us!

— *Address to Pilgrims From Naples*
(March 24, 1979)

For I resolved to know nothing while I was with you except Jesus Christ, and him crucified.

— 1 CORINTHIANS 2:2

40. CHRIST IS OUR PRAYER

As A MAN, the life of Jesus was a continual prayer, a continual act of worship and love of the Father, and since the maximum expression of prayer is sacrifice, the summit of Jesus' prayer is the Sacrifice of the Cross, anticipated with the Eucharist at the Last Supper and handed down with Holy Mass throughout the centuries.

Therefore, the Christian knows that his prayer is Jesus; every prayer of his starts from Jesus; it is he who prays in us, with us, for us.

All those who believe in God pray; but the Christian prays in Jesus Christ: Christ is our prayer!

— *Address to Young People*
(March 14, 1979)

"I pray for them. I do not pray for the world but for the ones you have given me, because they are yours, and everything of mine is yours and everything of yours is mine, and I have been glorified in them."

— JOHN 17:9-10

41. KNOW CHRIST

ALL THAT I CAN say to you is summed up in the words: *Get to know Christ and make yourselves known to him.* He knows each one of you in a particular way. It is not a knowledge made up of hypotheses and reducing man to his dimensions of social utility. The knowledge of Christ is *a knowledge full of the simple truth about "man" and, above all, full of love.* Submit yourselves to this simple and loving knowledge of the Good Shepherd. Be certain that he knows each one of you more than each one of you knows himself. He knows because he has laid down his life.

— *Address to University Students in Kraków, Poland*
(June 8, 1979)

"This is my commandment: love one another as I love you. No one has greater love than this, to lay down one's life for one's friends."
— JOHN 15:12-13

42. ALIVE IN CHRIST

"DYING TO SIN" AND "being alive to God in Christ Jesus" is a commitment for your whole life and it requires effort for the future. It means keeping yourselves free, by God's grace, from hatred and rancor. It means pardoning those who may have sinned against you. It means *being reconciled* to one another and to God, to forgiveness and love. But forgiveness is an act which is greater than our poor hearts: it belongs to God alone.

— *Homily, Mass in Kwangju, South Korea*
(May 4, 1984)

"Blessed are the merciful,
for they will be shown mercy."

— MATTHEW 5:7

43. ONE IN CHRIST

IT IS THIS GREAT mystery that we ponder each day in the *Angelus*: God became man in the womb of Mary.

Through this great mystery, all human life was changed. Humanity received a new dignity. God became one with us in all things but sin, so that we might become one with God. The moment Mary said yes — "Be it done unto me according to your word" — God came down to earth, and the life of every man and woman was lifted up. We human beings were brought close to God by God drawing near to us. But not only that — we were also brought closer to one another.

— *Angelus*
(February 2, 1986)

And the Word became flesh
  and made his dwelling among us,
  and we saw his glory,
  the glory as of the Father's only Son,
  full of grace and truth.

— JOHN 1:14

44. Close to Christ in Suffering

Dear sick brother or sister!

If someone or something makes you think that you have reached the end of the line, do not believe it! If you know the eternal Love who created you, you also know that there is an immortal soul within you. There are various seasons in life; if by chance you feel winter approaching, I want you to know that it is not the last season, because the last one will be spring: the springtime of the Resurrection. Your whole life extends infinitely beyond its earthly limits: heaven awaits you.

— *Greeting the Sick at Fátima, Portugal*
(May 13, 2000)

Therefore, we are not discouraged; rather, although our outer self is wasting away, our inner self is being renewed day by day. For this momentary light affliction is producing for us an eternal weight of glory beyond all comparison, as we look not to what is seen but to what is unseen; for what is seen is transitory, but what is unseen is eternal.

— 2 Corinthians 4:16-18

45. SEEING WITH NEW EYES

PRAYER TRANSFORMS OUR INDIVIDUAL lives and the life of the world. Young men and women, when you meet Christ in prayer, when you get to know his Gospel and reflect on it in relation to your hopes and your plans for the future, then *everything is new*. Everything is different when you begin to examine in prayer the circumstances of every day, according to the set of values that Jesus taught.... In prayer, united with Jesus — your brother, your friend, your Savior, your God — you begin to breathe a new atmosphere. You form new goals and new ideals. Yes, in Christ you begin to understand yourselves more fully.

— *Address to Youth of England and Wales*
(June 2, 1982)

Yet I live, no longer I, but Christ lives in me; insofar as I now live in the flesh, I live by faith in the Son of God who has loved me and given himself up for me.

— GALATIANS 2:20

46. HOW MUCH HE LOVES US

HOW CAN WE NOT be grateful to the Father who gives his own Son, his beloved Son with whom he is well pleased, placing in a creature's small womb the one whom the whole universe cannot contain? In the silence of the Holy Night, the mystery of Mary's divine motherhood reveals the radiant and welcoming face of the Father. His features of tender concern for the poor and sinners are already visible in the defenseless Child in the cave who lies in the arms of his Virgin Mother.

— *General Audience*
(December 23, 1998)

For God so loved the world that he gave his only Son, so that everyone who believes in him might not perish but might have eternal life.

— JOHN 3:16

47. A Gaze Transformed

THE MONK TURNS HIS gaze to Christ, God and man. In the disfigured face of Christ, the man of sorrow, he sees the prophetic announcement of the transfigured face of the Risen Christ. To the contemplative eye, Christ reveals himself as he did to the women of Jerusalem, who had gone up to contemplate the mysterious spectacle on Calvary. Trained in this school, the monk becomes accustomed to contemplating Christ in the hidden recesses of creation and in the history of mankind, which is then understood from the standpoint of identification with the whole Christ.

— *Orientale Lumen*, n. 12
(apostolic letter, May 2, 1995)

Then they went away quickly from the tomb, fearful yet overjoyed, and ran to announce this to his disciples. And behold, Jesus met them on their way and greeted them. They approached, embraced his feet, and did him homage.

— MATTHEW 28:8-9

48. Listen to the Word

In replying to the angel, "Let it be to me according to your word" (Luke 1:38) and in stating her readiness to fulfill perfectly the Lord's will, Mary rightly shares in the beatitude proclaimed by Jesus: "Blessed are those who hear the word of God and keep it!" (Luke 11:28).

With this attitude, which encompasses her entire life, the Blessed Virgin indicates the high road of listening to the Word of the Lord, an essential element of worship, which has become typical of the Christian liturgy. Her example shows us that worship does not primarily consist in expressing human thoughts and feelings, but in listening to the divine Word in order to know it, assimilate it, and put it into practice in daily life.

— *General Audience*
(September 10, 1997)

Your word is a lamp for my feet,
a light for my path.

— Psalm 119:105

49. HAVE COURAGE IN CHRIST

AND FINALLY, I TELL YOU, bear witness to Jesus with your courageous faith and your innocence.

It is no use complaining of the wickedness of the times. As St. Paul wrote, we must overcome evil by doing good (Romans 12:21). The world esteems and respects the courage of ideas and the strength of virtues. Do not be afraid to refuse words, acts, and attitudes which are not in conformity with Christian ideals. Be courageous in rejecting what destroys your innocence or wilts the freshness of your love for Christ.

— *Address to Youth*
(November 8, 1978)

Do not be conquered by evil but conquer evil with good.
— ROMANS 12:21

50. Sharing What We Have

BUT ALMS, IN ITSELF, must be understood essentially as the attitude of a man who perceives the need of others, who wishes to share his own property with others. Who will say that there will not always be another, in need of help — spiritual in the first place — support, comfort, brotherhood, and love? The world is always too poor in love.

... Even if we do not have at our disposal riches and concrete capacities to meet the needs of our neighbor, we cannot feel dispensed from opening our heart to his necessities and relieving them as far as possible. Remember the widow's mite; she threw into the treasury of the temple only two small coins but with them all her great love.

— *Address to Young People*
(March 28, 1979)

He said, "I tell you truly, this poor widow put in more than all the rest; for those others have all made offerings from their surplus wealth, but she, from her poverty, has offered her whole livelihood."

— LUKE 21:3-4

51. On the Way to God

We must think of Paradise! We play the card of our Christian life staking it on Paradise! This certainty and this expectation does not distract us from our earthly commitments; on the contrary, it purifies and intensifies them, as the lives of all the saints prove.

Our life is a path towards Paradise, where we will be loved and will love forever in a complete and perfect way. We are born only to go to Paradise.

The thought of Paradise must make you strong against temptations, committed to your religious and moral formation, watchful with regard to the environment in which you must live, confident that, if you are united with Christ, you will triumph over every difficulty.

— *Address to the Parish of San Basilio, Rome*
(March 11, 1979)

Therefore, since we are surrounded by so great a cloud of witnesses, let us rid ourselves of every burden and sin that clings to us and persevere in running the race that lies before us while keeping our eyes fixed on Jesus, the leader and perfecter of faith.

— Hebrews 12:1-2

52. LETTING GO

*T*O BE CONVERTED TO GOD, it is necessary to *discover in ourselves* that which makes us *sensitive to what belongs to God*; therefore, the spiritual contents, the superior values which speak to our intellect, to our conscience, to our "heart" (according to biblical language). To open up to these spiritual contents, to these values, it is necessary to detach oneself from what serves only the consumer spirit, satisfaction of the senses. In the opening of our human personality to God, fasting — understood both in the "traditional" way and in the "modern" way — must go hand in hand with prayer because it is addressed directly to him.

— *General Audience*
(March 21, 1979)

But Zacchaeus stood there and said to the Lord, "Behold, half of my possessions, Lord, I shall give to the poor, and if I have extorted anything from anyone I shall repay it four times over."

— LUKE 19:8

53. Share the Good News

At the dawn of Redemption, we can glimpse in the prophetess Anna all women who, with holiness of life and in prayerful expectation, are ready to accept Christ's presence and to praise God every day for the marvels wrought by his everlasting mercy.

Chosen to meet the Child, Simeon and Anna have a deep experience of sharing the joy of Jesus' presence with Mary and Joseph and spreading it where they live. Anna in particular shows wonderful zeal in speaking about Jesus, thus witnessing to her simple and generous faith. This faith prepares others to accept the Messiah in their lives.

— *General Audience*
(January 8, 1997)

There was also a prophetess, Anna. . . . And coming forward at that very time, she gave thanks to God and spoke about the child to all who were awaiting the redemption of Jerusalem.

— Luke 2:36, 38

54. GRATITUDE FOR THE GIFT

WHEN WE RECEIVE A GIFT, we are a debtor. Indeed we are more than a debtor because it is not possible to repay a gift adequately. And yet we must try. *We must give a gift in return for a gift.* God's generous gift must be repaid by our gift. And our gift, reflecting as it does our great limitations, must aim at imitating the divine generosity, the divine standard of giving. In Christ, our gift must be transformed, so as to unite us with God. The Eucharist is the sacrament of such a *transformation.* Christ himself makes us "an everlasting gift to the Father." Truly this is the great mystery of faith and love.

— *Homily, Mass in New Orleans*
(September 12, 1987)

And one of them, realizing he had been healed, returned, glorifying God in a loud voice; and he fell at the feet of Jesus and thanked him.
— LUKE 17:15-16

55. Open, Loving Hearts

LOVE IS THE FORCE that opens hearts to the word of Jesus and to his Redemption: love is the only basis for human relationships that respect in one another the dignity of the children of God created in his image and saved by the death and Resurrection of Jesus; love is the only driving force that impels us to share with our brothers and sisters all that we are and have.

Love is the power that gives rise to dialogue, in which we listen to each other and learn from each other. Love gives rise, above all, to the dialogue of prayer in which we listen to God's word, which is alive in the Holy Bible and alive in the life of the Church.

— *Homily, Mass in Chicago*
(October 5, 1979)

So faith, hope, love remain, these three; but the greatest of these is love.
— 1 CORINTHIANS 13:13

56. Christ Brings Good Out of Suffering

THIS INTERIOR MATURITY AND spiritual greatness in suffering are certainly the *result* of a particular *conversion* and cooperation with the grace of the Crucified Redeemer. It is he himself who acts at the heart of human sufferings through his Spirit of truth, through the consoling Spirit.... *It is he* — as the interior Master and Guide — *who reveals* to the suffering brother and sister this *wonderful interchange*, situated at the very heart of the mystery of the Redemption. Suffering is, in itself, an experience of evil. But Christ has made suffering the firmest basis of the definitive good, namely the good of eternal salvation.

— *Salvifici Doloros*, n. 26
(apostolic letter, February 11, 1984)

While they were eating, he took bread, said the blessing, broke it, and gave it to them, and said, "Take it; this is my body." Then he took a cup, gave thanks, and gave it to them, and they all drank from it. He said to them, "This is my blood of the covenant, which will be shed for many."

— MARK 14:22-24

57. Rejoice in the Lord's Day

Rightly, then, the Psalmist's cry is applied to Sunday: "This is the day which the Lord has made: let us rejoice and be glad in it" (Psalm 118:24). This invitation to joy, which the Easter liturgy makes its own, reflects the astonishment which came over the women who, having seen the crucifixion of Christ, found the tomb empty when they went there "very early on the first day after the Sabbath" (Mark 16:2). It is an invitation to relive in some way the experience of the two disciples of Emmaus, who felt their hearts "burn within them" as the Risen One walked with them on the road, explaining the Scriptures and revealing himself in "the breaking of the bread" (cf. Luke 24:32, 35).

— *Dies Domini*, n. 1
(apostolic letter, May 31, 1998)

This is the day the Lord has made;
let us rejoice in it and be glad.

— Psalm 118:24

58. JESUS TEACHES US HOW TO BE HUMAN

THE BIRTH OF JESUS at Bethlehem is not an event which can be consigned to the past. The whole of human history in fact stands in reference to him: our own time and the future of the world are illumined by his presence.... In the encounter with Christ, every man discovers the mystery of his own life.

... The Incarnation of the Son of God and the salvation which he has accomplished by his death and resurrection are therefore the true criterion for evaluating all that happens in time and every effort to make life more human.

— *Papal Bull Announcing the 2000 Jubilee*
(November 29, 1998)

He is the image of the invisible God,
the firstborn of all creation.

— COLOSSIANS 1:15

59. WE SEE GOD ON THE CROSS

HE SPOKE TO US of God, and perhaps with that one sentence of the prayer at Gethsemane, or with the seven words he spoke on the cross, he told us who God is even more than in the whole of the Gospel.

... The penetrating revelation of justice and, at the same time, of love, which is mercy! Justice, love, [and] mercy would have remained concepts without an ultimate and definitive content, if there had not been this Passion and this cross.

— *Angelus*
(April 8, 1979)

But Jesus cried out again in a loud voice, and gave up his spirit. And behold, the veil of the sanctuary was torn in two from top to bottom.
— MATTHEW 27:50-51

60. THE STRENGTH IN PRAYER

PRAYER IS AN INVISIBLE BOND, which unites the Communities of the faithful. It is a very strong and deep bond. The spiritual unity of the People of God is expressed in it.

... The gift of prayer, which I receive from so many brothers and sisters of mine, is a source of continual strengthening. Christ, who exhorted Peter, "strengthen your brethren" (Luke 22:3), based this exhortation on his own prayer. He said: "I have prayed for you that your faith may not fail" (Luke 22:32). And when the difficult moment came, he gave him that strengthening of which we read in the Acts of the Apostles: the Church prayed for Peter.

— *Angelus*
(July 8, 1979)

With all prayer and supplication, pray at every opportunity in the Spirit. To that end, be watchful with all perseverance and supplication for all the holy ones.

— EPHESIANS 6:18

61. ON THE WAY TO GOD

DESPITE THE LIMITATIONS BROUGHT on by age, I continue to enjoy life. For this I thank the Lord. It is wonderful to be able to give oneself to the very end for the sake of the Kingdom of God!

At the same time, I find great peace in thinking of the time when the Lord will call me: from life to life! And so I often find myself saying, with no trace of melancholy, a prayer recited by priests after the celebration of the Eucharist: *In hora mortis meae voca me, et iube me venire ad te* — at the hour of my death, call me and bid me come to you. This is the prayer of Christian hope, which in no way detracts from the joy of the present, while entrusting the future to God's gracious and loving care.

— *Letter to the Elderly*
(October 1, 1999)

You are my hope, Lord;
my trust, GOD, from my youth.
On you I depend since birth;
from my mother's womb you are my strength;
my hope in you never wavers.

— PSALM 71:5–6

62. Sacrifices for the Good

Fasting means putting a limit on so many desires, sometimes good ones, in order to have full mastery of oneself, to learn to control one's own instincts, to train the will in good. Acts of this kind were once known as "*fioretti*" (small acts of sacrifice).... They were and remain acts of renunciation, carried out for love of the Lord or of Our Lady, with a noble purpose to attain. They were and are a "sport," [an] indispensable training in order to be victorious in the competitions of the Spirit! Fasting, finally, means depriving oneself of something in order to meet the need of one's brother, becoming, in this way, [an] exercise of goodness, of charity.

— *Address to Young People*
(March 21, 1979)

"Amen, amen, I say to you, unless a grain of wheat falls to the ground and dies, it remains just a grain of wheat; but if it dies, it produces much fruit."

— John 12:24

63. WHY WE LIVE THIS WAY

LET THE WORLD KNOW that you have chosen the path of truth, goodness and compassion, honesty and love, pardon and reconciliation where necessary, and openness to all. Yes, the path of generosity, personal discipline, and prayer. And when someone asks why you live this way, you will answer: *"Because of my faith in Jesus Christ."*

You will need strength, but God will give you his grace. Grace is indeed the power of God that lights the path of your life towards "the life which is life indeed" [see 1 Timothy 6:19].

— *Address to Young People, Seoul, South Korea*
(May 6, 1984)

"Just so, your light must shine before others, that they may see your good deeds and glorify your heavenly Father."

— MATTHEW 5:16

64. The Kindness of God

In Nirmal Hriday, the mystery of human suffering meets the mystery of faith and love. And in this meeting, the deepest questions of human existence make themselves heard. The pain-filled body and spirit cries out: "Why? What is the purpose of suffering? Why must I die?" And the answer that comes, often in unspoken ways of kindness and compassion, is filled with honesty and faith: "I cannot fully answer all your questions; I cannot take away all your pain. But of this I am sure: God loves you with an everlasting love. You are precious in his sight. In him I love you too. For in God we are truly brothers and sisters."

> — *Address at Nirmal Hriday Ashram, an Apostolate of the Missionaries of Charity* (February 3, 1986)

"When you hold a lunch or a dinner, do not invite your friends or your brothers or your relatives or your wealthy neighbors, in case they may invite you back and you have repayment. Rather, when you hold a banquet, invite the poor, the crippled, the lame, the blind; blessed indeed will you be because of their inability to repay you."

> — Luke 14:12-14

65. THE GRACE OF BAPTISM

Baptism... is a grace given to the sinner, a grace which purifies us from sin and opens to us a new future. It is a bath which washes and regenerates. It is an anointing which conforms us to Christ — Priest, Prophet, and King. It is an enlightenment which illumines our path and gives it full meaning. It is a vestment of strength and perfection.... Baptism is the sign that God has joined us on our journey, that he makes our existence more beautiful, and that he transforms our history into a history of holiness.

— *Baptismal Vigil With Young People,*
World Youth Day, Paris (August 23, 1997)

We were indeed buried with him through baptism into death, so that, just as Christ was raised from the dead by the glory of the Father, we too might live in newness of life.

— ROMANS 6:4

66. LIVING IN THE SPIRIT

THOSE WHO LIVE "by the flesh" experience God's law as a burden, and indeed as a denial or at least a restriction of their own freedom. On the other hand, those who are impelled by love and "walk by the Spirit" (Galatians 5:16) and who desire to serve others find in God's Law the fundamental and necessary way in which to practice love as something freely chosen and freely lived out. Indeed, they feel an interior urge — a genuine "necessity" and no longer a form of coercion — not to stop at the minimum demands of the Law, but to live them in their "fullness."

— *Veritatis Splendor,* n. 18
(encyclical, August 6, 1993)

Be free, yet without using freedom as a pretext for evil, but as slaves of God.

— 1 PETER 2:16

67. GOD'S WILL BRINGS PEACE

THIS TURNING POINT IN the life of Peter came about at the initiative of Jesus, not at the initiative of Peter. Peter's attempt ends in failure; but when he fishes at Jesus' command, the nets are filled to the breaking point.

The same thing happens in the life of each of us. While it is true that we ourselves decide what paths we will take, our decisions will lead us to true joy and fulfillment only if they are in accordance with God's will....

The secret of the successful catch of fish is the obedience of Peter and his companions.

— *Address to Young People, Auckland, New Zealand*
(November 22, 1986)

So then, my beloved, obedient as you have always been, not only when I am present but all the more now when I am absent, work out your salvation with fear and trembling. For God is the one who, for his good purpose, works in you both to desire and to work.

— PHILIPPIANS 2:12-13

68. CONTEMPLATE THE FACE OF CHRIST

THE GOSPEL SCENE OF Christ's transfiguration, in which the three apostles Peter, James, and John appear entranced by the beauty of the Redeemer, can be seen as *an icon of Christian contemplation*. To look upon the face of Christ, to recognize its mystery amid the daily events and the sufferings of his human life, and then to grasp the divine splendor definitively revealed in the Risen Lord, seated in glory at the right hand of the Father: this is the task of every follower of Christ and therefore the task of each one of us.

— *Rosarium Virginis Mariae*, n. 9
(apostolic letter, October 16, 2002)

All of us, gazing with unveiled face on the glory of the Lord, are being transformed into the same image from glory to glory, as from the Lord who is the Spirit.

— 2 CORINTHIANS 3:18

69. Mary, the First Disciple

This woman of faith, Mary of Nazareth, the Mother of God, has been given to us as a model in our pilgrimage of faith. From Mary, we learn to surrender to God's will in all things. From Mary, we learn to trust even when all hope seems gone. From Mary, we learn to love Christ, her Son and the Son of God....

... Learn from her to be always faithful, to trust that God's word to you will be fulfilled, and that nothing is impossible with God. Turn to Mary frequently in your prayer "for never was it known that anyone who fled to her protection, implored her help, or sought her intercession was left unaided."

— *Homily, Mass at St. Matthew's Cathedral, Washington, DC* (October 6, 1979)

His mother said to the servers, "Do whatever he tells you."
— John 2:5

70. Praying Together

THE VALUE OF THE Liturgy of the Hours is enormous. Through it, all the faithful, but especially the clergy and religious, fulfill a role of prime importance: Christ's prayer goes on in the world. The Holy Spirit himself intercedes for God's people. The Christian community, with praise and thanksgiving, glorifies the wisdom, the power, the providence, and the salvation of our God.

In this prayer of praise we lift up our hearts to the Father of our Lord Jesus Christ, bringing with us the anguish and hopes, the joys and sorrows of all our brothers and sisters in the world.

— *Address, Morning Prayer at St. Patrick's Cathedral, New York City* (October 3, 1979)

"Again, [amen,] I say to you, if two of you agree on earth about anything for which they are to pray, it shall be granted to them by my heavenly Father. For where two or three are gathered together in my name, there am I in the midst of them."

— MATTHEW 18:19-20

71. OUR GIFT TO GOD

WHEN WE RECEIVE A gift, *we must respond with a gift*. We can only respond to the gift of God in Jesus Christ — his cross and resurrection — in the way that Paul responded — with *the gift of ourselves....*

St. Paul, and everyone like him, realizes that one can *never match or equal the value of God's gift of himself to us*. The only measure that applies is the measure of love. And love's measure, as St. Bernard says, is *to love without measure* (*De Diligendo Deo*, I, 1).

— *Homily, Mass in Detroit*
(September 19, 1987)

How can I repay the LORD
for all the good done for me?

— PSALM 116:12

72. God's Power in Suffering

Down through the centuries and generations it has been seen that *in suffering there is concealed* a particular *power that draws a person interiorly close to Christ*, a special grace. To this grace many saints, such as St. Francis of Assisi, St. Ignatius of Loyola, and others, owe their profound conversion. A result of such a conversion is not only that the individual discovers the salvific meaning of suffering but above all that he becomes a completely new person.... When this body is gravely ill, totally incapacitated, and the person is almost incapable of living and acting, all the more do interior *maturity and spiritual greatness* become evident, constituting a touching lesson to those who are healthy and normal.

— *Salvifici Doloros*, no. 26
(apostolic letter, February 11, 1984)

We are afflicted in every way, but not constrained; perplexed, but not driven to despair; persecuted, but not abandoned; struck down, but not destroyed; always carrying about in the body the dying of Jesus, so that the life of Jesus may also be manifested in our body.

— 2 Corinthians 4:8-10

73. TRUE SELF-FULFILLMENT

MAN ACHIEVES THIS FULFILLMENT of his destiny through the sincere gift of self, a gift which is made possible only through his encounter with God. It is in God that man finds full self-realization: *this is the truth revealed by Christ.* Man fulfills himself in God, who comes to meet him through his Eternal Son. Thanks to God's coming on earth, human time, which began at Creation, has reached its fullness. "The fullness of time" is in fact eternity, indeed, it is *the One who is eternal*, God himself. Thus, to enter into "the fullness of time" means to reach the end of time and to transcend its limits, in order to find time's fulfillment in the eternity of God.

— *Tertio Millennio Adveniente*, n. 9
(apostolic letter, November 10, 1994)

The woman left her water jar and went into the town and said to the people, "Come see a man who told me everything I have done. Could he possibly be the Messiah?"

— JOHN 4:28-29

74. CHRISTLIKE HUMILITY

WE ARE OFTEN FASCINATED by apparent values, by exterior grandeur, by what is sensational, what agitates the surface of our psyche. Man becomes, in a certain sense, one-dimensional, detached from his own depth. He builds on foundations that are not deep. And he often suffers at the destruction of what he has built in himself so superficially. Lent calls for a deepening of our internal construction. And it is just this that gives rise to the call to humility, a virtue so significant in the whole Gospel message, the virtue so characteristic of Christ.

— *Angelus*
(March 4, 1979)

"If I, therefore, the master and teacher, have washed your feet, you ought to wash one another's feet. I have given you a model to follow, so that as I have done for you, you should also do."

— JOHN 13:14-15

75. GLIMPSES OF GOD

ALL ARTISTS EXPERIENCE THE unbridgeable gap which lies between the work of their hands, however successful it may be, and the dazzling perfection of the beauty glimpsed in the ardor of the creative moment: what they manage to express in their painting, their sculpting, their creating, is no more than a glimmer of the splendor which flared for a moment before the eyes of their spirit.

Believers find nothing strange in this: they know that they have had a momentary glimpse of the abyss of light which has its original wellspring in God.... If the intimate reality of things is always "beyond" the powers of human perception, how much more so is God in the depths of his unfathomable mystery!

— *Letter to Artists*
(April 4, 1999)

At present we see indistinctly, as in a mirror, but then face to face. At present I know partially; then I shall know fully, as I am fully known.
— 1 CORINTHIANS 13:12

76. LOOK FOR AND LISTEN TO JESUS

WHEN ONE IS REALLY convinced that Jesus is the Word Incarnate and is still present in the Church, then one accepts his
"word" completely, because it is a divine word which does not
deceive, which does not contradict itself, and which gives us
the true and only meaning of life and eternity. He alone, in
fact, has words of eternal life! He alone is the way, the truth,
and the life!

... To look for Jesus personally, with the eagerness and joy
of discovering the truth, gives deep inner satisfaction and great
spiritual strength in order then to put into practice what he
demands, even though it costs sacrifice.

— *Address to Youth*
(November 8, 1978)

In the beginning was the Word,
and the Word was with God,
and the Word was God.

— JOHN 1:1

77. THE LIGHT SHINES IN THE DARKNESS

Yet, in spite of the grief that sometimes penetrates into our lives, Christmas is a ray of light for all, because it reveals to us God's love and makes us feel the presence of Jesus with everyone, especially with those who are suffering. Just for this reason Jesus willed to be born in poverty and in the abandonment of a cave and to be laid in a manger.

There comes into my mind spontaneously the memory of my feelings and of my experiences, beginning with the years of my childhood in my father's house, through the difficult years of youth, the period of the second war, the world war. Yet even in the worst years, Christmas always brought some ray with it. And this ray penetrated even into the harshest experiences of contempt for man, destruction of his dignity, and cruelty.

— *Address to Young People*
(December 27, 1998)

What came to be through him was life,
    and this life was the light of the human race;
the light shines in the darkness
    and the darkness has not overcome it.

— John 1:3-5

78. TRUE PEACE

[MARY] UNDERSTANDS SINFUL MAN and loves him with a mother's love. Precisely for this reason she is on the side of truth and shares the Church's burden in recalling always and to everyone the demands of morality. Nor does she permit sinful man to be deceived by those who claim to love him by justifying his sin, for she knows that the sacrifice of Christ her Son would thus be emptied of its power. No absolution offered by beguiling doctrines, even in the areas of philosophy and theology, can make man truly happy: only the cross and the glory of the Risen Christ can grant peace to his conscience and salvation to his life.

— *Veritatis Splendor*, n. 120
(encyclical, August 6, 1993)

See to it that no one captivate you with an empty, seductive philosophy according to human tradition, according to the elemental powers of the world and not according to Christ.

— COLOSSIANS 2:8

79. A Missionary Heart

The missionary is required to "renounce himself and everything that up to this point he considered as his own, and to make himself everything to everyone" (*Ad Gentes*, n. 24). This he does by a poverty which sets him free for the Gospel, overcoming attachment to the people and things about him, so that he may become a brother to those to whom he is sent and thus bring them Christ the Savior. This is the goal of missionary spirituality.... It is precisely because he is "sent" that the missionary experiences the consoling presence of Christ, who is with him at every moment of life... and who awaits him in the heart of every person.

— *Redemptoris Missio*, n. 88
(encyclical, December 7, 1990)

To the weak I became weak, to win over the weak. I have become all things to all, to save at least some. All this I do for the sake of the gospel, so that I too may have a share in it.

— 1 Corinthians 9:22-23

80. THE GIFT OF AN OPEN HEART

THE MAGI KINGS, at the moment when they present themselves before the Child in his mother's arms, accept in the light
of the Epiphany the Gift of God Incarnate, his ineffable dedi-
cation to man in the mystery of the Incarnation. At the same
time, "opening their treasures, they offered him gifts" [Mat-
thew 2:11]; it is a question of the concrete gifts of which the
evangelist speaks, but above all they open themselves up to
him, with the interior gift of their own heart. And this is the
real treasure they offer, of which the gold, incense, and myrrh
are only an exterior expression. The fruit of the Epiphany con-
sists in this gift: they recognize God and they meet him.

— *General Audience*
(January 24, 1979)

*I urge you therefore, brothers, by the mercies of God, to offer your bodies
as a living sacrifice, holy and pleasing to God, your spiritual worship.*
— ROMANS 12:1

81. MEETING GOD IN SOLITUDE

THAT SHUTTING-IN OF ONESELF IS, at the same time, the deepest opening of the human heart. It is indispensable for the purpose of meeting the Father, and must be undertaken for this purpose. "Your Father who sees in secret will reward you" [Matthew 6:6]. Here it is a question of acquiring again the simplicity of thought, of will, and of heart which is indispensable to meet God in one's own "self." And God is waiting for that, in order to approach man who is absorbed interiorly and at the same time open to his word and his love!

— *General Audience*
(February 28, 1979)

"But when you pray, go to your inner room, close the door, and pray to your Father in secret. And your Father who sees in secret will repay you."

— MATTHEW 6:6

82. Finding God in Work

TRADITION, IN PARTICULAR, has seen [St. Joseph] as *the worker.*
"Is not this the carpenter's son?" (Matthew 13:55), the inhabit-
ants of Nazareth exclaim when they see the miracles worked
by Jesus. For them he is first and foremost the village carpenter, who expresses himself in work, fulfilling himself in God's
sight by serving his brothers and sisters. The Christian community has also considered the life of St. Joseph as exemplary
for all who are involved in the vast and complex world of work.

. . . The figure of St. Joseph recalls the urgent need to give a
soul to the world of work. His life, marked by listening to God
and by familiarity with Christ, appears as *a harmonious synthesis
of faith and life,* of personal fulfillment and love for one's brothers and sisters, of daily commitment and of trust in the future.

— *General Audience*
(March 19, 1997)

Good and upright is the LORD,
who shows sinners the way,
Guides the humble rightly,
and teaches the humble the way.

— PSALM 25:8-9

83. Hearing God in the Baby's Cry

NOWHERE WAS THERE ROOM. From the beginning, the world showed itself inhospitable towards the God who was to be born as Man.

On this night let us therefore think ... of those who are lonely, old, or sick; of the homeless, those suffering from hunger, and those whose misery is the result of the exploitation and injustice of economic systems.

... The stable at Bethlehem is the first place for solidarity with man: for one man's solidarity with another and for all men's with all men, especially with those for whom there is "no room at the inn" (cf. Luke 2:7), whose personal rights are refused recognition.

The newborn Infant is wailing. Who hears the baby's wail?

— *Homily, Midnight Mass*
(December 24, 1978)

For you know the gracious act of our Lord Jesus Christ, that for your sake he became poor although he was rich, so that by his poverty you might become rich.

— 2 CORINTHIANS 8:9

84. GLAD TIDINGS FOR THE LOWLY

FOR GOD'S JUSTICE AND PEACE cry out to bear fruit in human works of justice and peace, in all the spheres of actual life. When we Christians make Jesus Christ the center of our feelings and thoughts, we do not turn away from people and their needs. On the contrary, we are caught up in the eternal movement of God's love that comes to meet us; we are caught up in the movement of the Son, who came among us, who became one of us; we are caught up in the movement of the Holy Spirit, who visits the poor, calms fevered hearts, binds up wounded hearts, warms cold hearts, and gives us the fullness of his gifts.

— *Homily, Mass at Yankee Stadium, New York City* (October 2, 1979)

> *The spirit of the Lord GOD is upon me,*
> *because the LORD has anointed me;*
> *He has sent me to bring glad tidings to the lowly,*
> *to heal the brokenhearted....*

— ISAIAH 61:1

85. LOVE ETERNAL

As HE FACES DEATH, the human being has precisely this fear of being lost. His heart trembles, every certainty becomes precarious and the darkness of the unknown throws him into dismay.

The word of Christ then becomes the only key to unlocking the enigma of death. It is the light that illumines the way of life and gives value to its every moment, even to pain, suffering, and extreme detachment.... To believe in him is to trust in his words, relying solely on the power of his merciful love.

— *Homily, Funeral Mass for Cardinal Eduardo Francisco Pironio*
(February 7, 1998)

"And this is the will of the one who sent me, that I should not lose anything of what he gave me, but that I should raise it [on] the last day."
— JOHN 6:39

86. TURN TO THE LORD

WHAT IS PENANCE, if not a humble and sincere return to the sources of faith, by promptly rejecting temptation and sin and increasing our prayerful intimacy with the Lord?

Indeed, Christ alone can free man from what enslaves him to evil and selfishness: from the frantic search for material possessions, from the thirst for power and control over others and over things, from the illusion of easy success, from the frenzy of consumerism and hedonism which ultimately destroy the human being.

— *Homily, Pastoral Visit to the Parish of St. Agapitus in Rome*
(March 1, 1998)

If you confess with your mouth that Jesus is Lord and believe in your heart that God raised him from the dead, you will be saved.

— ROMANS 10:9

87. HIDDEN WITH CHRIST

A SETTING FOR GROWTH IN faith and hope, the house of Nazareth becomes a place of lofty witness to charity. The love that Christ wanted to pour forth in the world is kindled and burns first of all in his mother's heart: it is precisely in the home that the proclamation of the Gospel of divine love is prepared.

It is often a life that seems humble and obscure in the world's eyes, but which, following Mary's example, can reveal unexpected possibilities of salvation, radiating the love and peace of Christ.

— *General Audience*
(January 29, 1997)

For you have died, and your life is hidden with Christ in God. When Christ your life appears, then you too will appear with him in glory.
— COLOSSIANS 3:3-4

88. GOD IS GOOD

TODAY WE ARE CELEBRATING the memorial of St. Agatha, martyred in Catania, probably during the persecution of Decius in the third century. Agatha means "good." ... She is good to her Spouse, Christ, and good also to us through sharing with us her goodness....

God, our supreme good, is the source of all good things. I hope that you will all be "good," that is, faithful witnesses to the love of our heavenly Father who fills us with so many gifts and calls us to share in his own joy.

— General Audience
(February 5, 1997)

Be at peace among yourselves.

We urge you, brothers, admonish the idle, cheer the fainthearted, support the weak, be patient with all.

— 1 THESSALONIANS 5:13-14

89. THE NAME OF JESUS

DEAR BROTHERS AND SISTERS: the name of Jesus, like the Word of God that he is, is a two-edged sword. *It is a name that means salvation and life*; it is a name that means a struggle and a cross, just as it did for him. But it is also the name in which we find *strength to proclaim and live the truth* of the Gospel: not with arrogance, but with confident joy; not with self-righteousness, but with humble repentance before God.

— *Address*, Cathedral of St. Vibiana, Los Angeles
(September 15, 1987)

Indeed, the word of God is living and effective, sharper than any two-edged sword, penetrating even between soul and spirit, joints and marrow, and able to discern reflections and thoughts of the heart.

— HEBREWS 4:12

90. HE REDEEMS US

AT ANY RATE, CHRIST drew close above all to the world of human suffering through the fact of having taken *this suffering upon his very self*. During his public activity, he experienced not only fatigue, homelessness, misunderstanding even on the part of those closest to him, but, more than anything, he became progressively more and more isolated and encircled by hostility and the preparations for putting him to death.... Christ goes towards his Passion and death with full awareness of the mission that he has to fulfill precisely in this way. Precisely *by means of this suffering* he must bring it about "that man should not perish, but have eternal life" [cf. John 3:16].

— *Salvifici Doloros*, n. 16
(apostolic letter, February 11, 1984)

He himself bore our sins in his body upon the cross, so that, free from sin, we might live for righteousness. By his wounds you have been healed.

— 1 PETER 2:24

91. WORD MADE FLESH

JESUS DOES NOT IN FACT merely speak "in the name of God" like the prophets, but he is God himself speaking in his Eternal Word made flesh. Here we touch upon *the essential point by which Christianity differs from all the other religions*, by which *man's search for God* has been expressed from earliest times. Christianity has its starting point in the Incarnation of the Word. Here, it is not simply a case of man seeking God, but of God who comes in Person to speak to man of himself and to show him the path by which he may be reached.

— *Tertio Millennio Adveniente*, n. 6
(apostolic letter, November 10, 1994)

No one has ever seen God. The only Son, God, who is at the Father's side, has revealed him.

— JOHN 1:18

92. Becoming Like Christ

This gaze progressively conformed to Christ thus learns detachment from externals, from the tumult of the senses, from all that keeps man from that freedom which allows him to be grasped by the Spirit. Walking this path, he is reconciled with Christ in a constant process of conversion: in the awareness of his own sin and of his distance from the Lord which becomes heartfelt remorse, a symbol of his own baptism in the salutary water of tears; in silence and inner quiet, which is sought and given, where he learns to make his heart beat in harmony with the rhythm of the Spirit, eliminating all duplicity and ambiguity.

— *Orientale Lumen*, n. 12
(apostolic letter, May 2, 1995)

Have among yourselves the same attitude that is also yours in Christ Jesus.

— Philippians 2:5

93. THE SCHOOL OF CHARITY

LIVED IN THIS WAY, not only the Sunday Eucharist but the whole of Sunday becomes a great school of charity, justice, and peace. The presence of the Risen Lord in the midst of his people becomes an undertaking of solidarity, a compelling force for inner renewal, an inspiration to change the structures of sin in which individuals, communities, and at times entire peoples are entangled. Far from being an escape, the Christian Sunday is a "prophecy" inscribed on time itself, a prophecy obliging the faithful to follow in the footsteps of the One who came "to preach good news to the poor, to proclaim release to captives and new sight to the blind, to set at liberty those who are oppressed, and to proclaim the acceptable year of the Lord" (Luke 4:18-19).

— *Dies Domini*, n. 73
(apostolic letter, May 31, 1998)

"Amen, I say to you, whatever you did for one of these least brothers of mine, you did for me."

— MATTHEW 25:40

94. PEACE ON THE JOURNEY

GRANT, O LORD OF LIFE, that we may be ever vividly aware of this and that we may savor every season of our lives as a gift filled with promise for the future.

... And when the moment of our definitive "passage" comes, grant that we may face it with serenity, without regret for what we shall leave behind. For in meeting you, after having sought you for so long, we shall find once more every authentic good which we have known here on earth, in the company of all who have gone before us marked with the sign of faith and hope.

— *Letter to the Elderly*
(June 8, 1979)

"Now, Master, you may let your servant go
in peace, according to your word,
for my eyes have seen your salvation."

— LUKE 2:29-30

95. God Seeks

Allow him to find you. A human being, a young person, at times gets lost in himself, in the world about him, and in all the network of human affairs that wrap him round. Allow Christ to find you. Let him know all about you and guide you. It is true that following someone requires also *making demands on ourselves.* That is the law of friendship. If we wish to travel together, we must pay attention to the road we are to take. If we go walking in the mountains, we must follow the signs. If we go mountain climbing, we cannot let go of the rope. We must also preserve our unity with the Divine Friend whose name is Jesus Christ. We must cooperate with him.

— *Address to University Students in Kraków, Poland*
(June 8, 1979)

"For the Son of Man has come to seek and to save what was lost."
— Luke 19:10

96. He Knows Us

AND HE, JESUS, tells us how to live, because he tells us why we are alive. Jesus explains to us our origin, our life, our destiny. We have been created by God, and in Jesus we are children of God; we have come forth from God's love. We are here to know God, to love [him] and to serve him — to discover, embrace, and minister to him in our neighbor. And our destiny is to live with him forever. In his Gospel, Jesus explains these truths to us and, in the light of these truths, he explains what is expected of us in life....

In a word, Jesus explains us to ourselves.

— *Address to Youth in Bombay (Mumbai), India*
(February 10, 1986)

"My sheep hear my voice; I know them, and they follow me."
— JOHN 10:27

97. Our Home Is in the Lord

WE ALL HAVE OUR personal history and an innate desire to see God, a desire which makes itself felt at the same time as we discover the created world. This world is wonderful and rich; it sets before us countless treasures; it enchants us; it attracts both our reason and our will. But in the end it does not satisfy our spirit....

... We discover our vocation and develop our personality throughout our years of activity; then the moment comes when we must leave this world. The longer we live, the more we realize how precarious life is, and the more we wonder about immortality: what exists beyond the frontiers of death? Then, from the depths of our being, there arises the same question asked of the one who conquered death: "Rabbi, where are you staying?" [John 1:38].

— *Homily, Mass for World Youth Day, Paris* (August 24, 1997)

"Come," says my heart, "seek God's face";
  your face, LORD, do I seek!
Do not hide your face from me.

— PSALM 27:8-9

LISTENING TO GOD WITH BLESSED JOHN PAUL II   107

98. CONTEMPLATING CHRIST

NO ONE HAS EVER devoted himself to the contemplation of the face of Christ as faithfully as Mary....

... Mary's gaze, ever filled with adoration and wonder, would never leave him. At times it would be *a questioning look*, as in the episode of the finding in the Temple: ... it would always be *a penetrating gaze*, one capable of deeply understanding Jesus, even to the point of perceiving his hidden feelings and anticipating his decisions, as at Cana. At other times it would be *a look of sorrow*, especially beneath the cross.... On the morning of Easter hers would be *a gaze radiant with the joy of the Resurrection*, and finally, on the day of Pentecost, *a gaze afire* with the outpouring of the Spirit.

— *Rosarium Virginis Mariae*, n. 10
(apostolic letter, October 16, 2002)

He went down with them and came to Nazareth, and was obedient to them; and his mother kept all these things in her heart.

— LUKE 2:51

99. THE SIGN OF THE CROSS

THE CROSS IS THE sign of the deepest humiliation of Christ. In the eyes of the people of that time, it was the sign of an infamous death. Free men could not be punished with such a death, only slaves. Christ willingly accepts this death, death on the cross. Yet this death becomes the beginning of the Resurrection. In the Resurrection, the crucified Servant of Yahweh is lifted up: he is lifted up before the whole of creation.

At the same time, the cross is also lifted up. It ceases to be the sign of infamous death and becomes the sign of resurrection, that is, of life.

— *Homily, Mass in Halifax, Canada*
(September 14, 1984)

. . . He humbled himself,
becoming obedient to death,
*   even death on a cross.*

— PHILIPPIANS 2:8

100. SACRED HEART

THE HEART OF JESUS was conceived beneath the heart of the Virgin Mother, and its earthly life ceased at the moment Jesus died on the cross. This is testified to by the Roman soldier who pierced the side of Jesus with a lance.

... What constitutes the greatest fruit of this love in creation?

... Here is the most magnificent, the most profound gift of the Heart of Jesus that we find in creation: man born of God, man adopted as a son in the Eternal Son, humanity given the power to become children of God.

— *Homily, Mass in Vancouver, Canada*
(September 18, 1984)

We love because he first loved us.

— 1 JOHN 4:19

ABOUT THE COMPILER

AMY WELBORN is the author of many books, including these Our Sunday Visitor titles: *Prove It* series, *Here. Now. A Catholic Guide to the Good Life*, and *De-coding Mary Magdalene*. She lives in Birmingham, Alabama. Her website is *www.amywelborn.com*.

LISTENING TO GOD ...
FROM
OUR SUNDAY VISITOR

Listening to God with Padre Pio
(Inventory No. T1188)

Listening to God with Mother Teresa
(Inventory No. T1094)

OUR SUNDAY VISITOR
1-800-348-2440
WWW.OSV.COM